THE GINGERBREAD MAN

A musical play

DAVID WOOD

SAMUEL FRENCH

LONDON

NEW YORK TORONTO SYDNEY HOLLYWOOD

ISBN 0 573 05042 2

Printed in Great Britain by Butler & Tanner Ltd, Frome and London

To Katherine Emily—
the first play she saw

The Gingerbread Man

Originally commissioned by the Towngate Theatre, Basildon, and produced there by the Theatre Royal, Norwich (Trust) Ltd., on the 7th December 1976, with the following cast of characters:

Herr Von Cuckoo	Ronnie Stevens
Salt	Tim Barker
Pepper	Pearly Gates
The Gingerbread Man	Jack Chissick
The Old Bag	Veronica Clifford
Sleek, The Mouse	Keith Varnier

The play directed by Jonathan Lynn
Setting and costumes by Susie Caulcutt
Musical direction by Peter Pontzen
Lighting by Martyn Wills

The action of the play takes place on a kitchen dresser.

ACT I At Night
ACT II Immediately following

CHARACTERS

Herr Von Cuckoo: The Swiss-made cuckoo in the cuckoo clock. He wears leder-hosen.

Salt: A salt cellar, based in design on the blue-and-white horizontal striped variety, thus making him look like a sailor, and indeed that's how he sees himself.

Pepper: A well-groomed, svelte, elegant female pepper-mill.

The Gingerbread Man: Who looks like what he is!

The Old Bag: An elderly, short-tempered, tea bag, who lives on the shelf, inside a cottage-style teapot.

Sleek, The Mouse: An American gangster-style villain. Not as smooth as he'd like to appear.

The Voices of The Big Ones: These can either be pre-recorded or doubled by other members of the cast. They are the voices of the family who own the house in whose kitchen and on whose dresser the action takes place.

AUTHOR'S NOTE

As this is a musical play, not a pantomime, it helps if all the cast play their lines and situations for truth and reality (even though their characters may seem to belong in the realm of fantasy!), rather than adopt a superficial, 'knowing' style of performance often associated, sadly, with panto. The original production of this play proved that audience participation and involvement works best when it is motivated by genuine concern for the characters and their problems; and this concern is created by the *cast's* genuine concern for them.

David Wood

MUSICAL NUMBERS

ACT I

No.	Title	Performers
1.	Toad in the Throat	Herr Von Cuckoo
2.	The Dresser Hop	Salt, Pepper, Herr Von Cuckoo
3.	The Gingerbread Man	The Gingerbread Man, Salt, Pepper, Herr Von Cuckoo
4.	Beware of the Old Bag	Salt, Pepper, Herr Von Cuckoo
5.	Heave-Ho, A-Rolling Go	Salt, Pepper, The Gingerbread Man
6.	The Power of the Leaf	The Old Bag, The Gingerbread Man
7.	Sleek the Mouse	Sleek the Mouse

Interval

ACT II

No.	Title	Performers
7A.	Heave-Ho, A-Rolling Go (reprise)	Salt, Pepper, The Gingerbread Man
8.	Herbal Remedy	The Old Bag, Salt, Pepper, The Gingerbread Man
9.	Hot Stuff	Pepper
10.	Come the Light	Salt, Pepper, The Gingerbread Man, The Old Bag
10A.	Toad in the Throat (reprise)	Herr Von Cuckoo, Audience, *with* Salt, Pepper, the Gingerbread Man, The Old Bag
10B.	The Gingerbread Man (reprise)	All (except Sleek the Mouse)

The piano/vocal score for this play is available from
Samuel French Ltd

ACT I*

The action of the play takes place on a kitchen dresser. The characters are all but inches high; therefore the set is magnified. It is one structure, which remains throughout the play

The stage surface is the "top" of the dresser, in other words the working surface. The edge of the stage can therefore be the edge of the dresser. Positioned, say, 12 or 15 feet upstage is the back of the dresser, incorporating one practical shelf, and hopefully the beginnings of another (non-practical) shelf. Naturally at stage surface level there is a "shelf-like area", under the practical shelf above. On the "lower" shelf are two plates standing upright, one of which is practical in that it slides to one side to reveal a hole in the wooden back of the dresser, through which Sleek the Mouse enters; the other is practical in that it is used in the action to put things on. There is also a practical mug. There are several hooks along the edge of the shelf. There is also a length of string, which could be in a tin, or just the remains of an opened parcel; also a sugar bowl, with several practical lumps of sugar; and an egg cup. A gaily-coloured pocket transistor radio can be either suspended from another hook, or horizontal on the top surface. On the "upper" (practical) shelf is a cottage-style teapot. It has a practical front door. Next to it are various herb jars, which never move, but could have lids. There is a pot of honey. Other larger jars could be visible (probably painted, or simply the front facades). Beside or in the middle of the shelved part of the dresser, is a cuckoo clock, with a practical door. Herr Von Cuckoo should be able to reach from his cuckooing podium to the dresser working surface, perhaps by swinging on the short end of the pendulum or by having a pendulum with rungs, like a ladder. But as two characters have to make the return journey—i.e. from dresser to clock, it may be more feasible to make the "podium" a sort of balcony, reachable by stepping up from the working surface. On the working surface itself sits a rolling pin. A tea-cloth is somewhere handy. Other dresser clutter could be visible—non-practical fixed "dresser dressing"! This could extend up to a non-practical top shelf, which could extend into the flies; or the very top of the dresser could be visible

The set is backed by black tabs, and hopefully a floor cloth, with the dresser surface painted on; this should have black surrounds extending from the surface edges to the wings, thus truly defining the working area. If possible, a front cloth could be used instead of tabs. This would have the show's title and possibly a gingerbread man motif, plus a design of the dresser (on its own or as part of a kitchen scene). This could help the establishing of the large scale set

If an overture is required, it is suggested that a verse and chorus of Toad in the Throat *be played*

As the CURTAIN *rises we hear the ticking of the cuckoo clock, the hands of which point to twelve o'clock. The dresser is revealed in lighting which suggests*

---

* N.B. Paragraph 3 on page ii of this Acting Edition regarding photocopying and video-recording should be carefully read.

moonlight, though it must obviously be bright enough to see everything clearly, as this will be the basic lighting for most of the play. Salt and Pepper stand, respectively back and front to the audience, under the practical shelf. An envelope stands between them, leaning against Pepper. Salt and Pepper are in frozen positions. Suddenly the door of the cuckoo clock opens, and Herr Von Cuckoo enters. Rather ostentatiously he clears his throat

Herr Von Cuckoo: (*warming up*) Mi, mi, mi, mi. (*He looks up at the clock face to check the time, and launches into his rhythmic twelve-cuckoo-call*) Cuckoo! Cuckoo! Cuckoo! Cuckoo! (*The first four are confident and perky. Between each one he nods or turns his head in a clockwork manner. He keeps count on his fingers. Under his breath*) Vier. Four. (*He carries on*) Cuckoo! Cuckoo! Cuckoo! Cuckoo! (*During the second four, it becomes a bit of an effort, breathing-wise and counting-wise. Under his breath*) Er—acht. Eight. (*He carries on*) Cuckoo! Cuck-oo! (*breath*) Cuck-oo! Cu—ck—oooooh. (*The sound changes into one of disgust. During the last four he has developed a husky frog in the throat, and it is a real strain to get the sound out. He tries clearing his throat. A very husky note*) Aaaah. What a noise horrible, nicht war? Hoppla! Ich ze toad in ze throat have. (*He tries a scale, but it cracks up nastily*) Doh, ray, me, fah, so—(*repeating*)—fah—so—fah so... (*Speaking*) So far so no good! (*singing*) La—(*straining*)—te... (*He tries 'doh', but nothing comes out; he has to go back down the octave to the lower 'doh'*) DOH! (*He sighs*) Oh...

Song 1 TOAD IN THE THROAT

Herr Von Cuckoo I was made in the mountains of Switzerland
(*yodel*)
From a fine piece of pine I was carved by hand
(*yodel*)
With all
My power
I call
The hour
On a clear and unwavering note
But I
Declare
To my
Despair
Today I've a toad in my throat.

(*yodelling chorus*)

'Cross the valleys of Switzerland you can hear
(*yodel*)
It's the sound of a yodelling mountaineer
(*yodel*)
He's all
Alone

Can't call
By 'phone
On a mountainside high and remote
When in
Distress
He's in
A mess
If he gets a toad in his throat.
(*half chorus of yodelling*)
Oh dear, oh dear
What can I do
I'm a cuckoo clock cuckoo who can't cuckoo.

So before people notice there's something wrong
(*husky yodel*)
I must try to recover my cuckoo song
(*husky yodel*)
A Swiss
You'll find
Is dis-
Inclined
To let a thing get on his goat
So I
Won't rest
I'll try
My best
To banish this toad from my throat.

After the song, Herr Von Cuckoo shakes his head, checks to see that all is clear, then locks his door and, pocketing the key, makes his way onto the dresser. He arrives near Salt and Pepper. Salt is nearest him. Both are asleep

Herr Von Cuckoo (*in a husky whisper*) Herr Salt. (*He tries to speak louder but cannot*) Herr Salt. (*Giving up, he goes round to Pepper. He stands three paces from her*) Fraulein Pepper. (*He moves in to her*)

Pepper wakes and starts to sneeze

Pepper A—A—A ...
Herr Von Cuckoo Bitte...
Pepper Tishoo!

Pepper's sneeze sends him reeling back. He tries again

A—A—A ...
Herr Von Cuckoo Entschuldigen-Sie...
Pepper Tishoo!

Again Herr Von Cuckoo reels back. He tries again

A—A—A ...
Herr Von Cuckoo Fraulein ...

Deftly he pulls out a handkerchief and puts it to her nose in the nick of time. This successfully stops the "Tishoo". Pepper holds in her breath.
Herr Von Cuckoo waits a moment, checks to see he has stopped it, removes the handkerchief and meticulously starts to fold it and put it in his pocket

Pepper (*just when Herr Von Cuckoo least expects it*) Tishoo!

Herr Von Cuckoo jumps. Pepper wakes up

What's going on? Oh, Herr Von Cuckoo, it's you.
Herr Von Cuckoo (*huskily*) Ja. Guten tag.

Herr Von Cuckoo shakes her hand and kisses her on both cheeks

Pepper Cuckoo, please! You'll knock me over. (*She becomes aware of the envelope leaning against her*) Oh no, the Big Ones have done it again. (*Calling*) Mr Salt. Mr Salt.

The envelope is now leaning on Salt. He wakes up

Salt Shiver me timbers! Storm to starboard! Ready about! Man the life-boats! We're running aground! S.O.S.! (*He keeps the envelope from falling on him as he turns to face the audience*)
Pepper All right! It's all right, Mr Salt. Wake up. We're not running aground. You were having one of your nautical nightmares.
Salt Sorry, Miss Pepper. I dreamed the windblown sails were enveloping us.
Pepper No, Mr Salt, we are being enveloped by an envelope. Kindly remove it.
Salt Ah. Aye, aye, ma'am. (*He salutes and starts to struggle with it*)
Pepper I refuse to be used as a letter rack.

Herr Von Cuckoo helps with the envelope

Salt Thank you, shipmate. We'll anchor it here. Couldn't have heave-hoed it on my own. Might have spliced my mainbrace. Ha, ha. Good morrow to you! (*He salutes*)
Herr Von Cuckoo (*huskily*) Guten tag.

Herr Von Cuckoo shakes Salt's hands and kisses him on both cheeks

Salt Aye, aye. (*Rather embarrassed*) Aye, aye! What can we do for you, shipmate?

Sadly, Herr Von Cuckoo points to his mouth and opens and shuts it

Speak up. Don't be shy. (*To Pepper*) What's he doing? Looks fishy to me! (*He opens and shuts* his *mouth*)
Pepper Maybe he's hungry.
Salt (*to Herr Von Cuckoo*) Are you hungry?
Herr Von Cuckoo (*whispering*) Nein. Ich need your 'elp.
Salt (*whispering*) What?
Herr Von Cuckoo (*whispering*) Ich need your 'elp.

Pepper (*to Salt*) What?
Salt (*to Pepper, whispering*) Ich need your 'elp.
Pepper (*in normal voice*) Why?
Salt (*whispering*) I don't know.
Pepper No. I mean ask *him* why.
Salt (*to Herr Von Cuckoo whispering*) Why?
Herr Von Cuckoo (*whispering*) Ich have ein difficulty.
Salt (*to Pepper, whispering*) Ich have ein difficulty.
Pepper What are you whispering for?
Salt (*to Herr Von Cuckoo, whispering*) What are you whispering...
Pepper No, no, I'm asking *you*. What are *you* whispering for?
Salt I don't know.
Pepper Then don't.
Salt I won't.
Pepper Now, what is your difficulty?
Salt Well, I keep whispering.
Pepper No, no. Ask *him*, "What is your difficulty?" My, you're stupid.
Salt (*to Herr Von Cuckoo*) What is your difficulty? My, you're stupid.
Pepper No!
Salt No!
Pepper Out of the way.
Salt I'm sorry, ma'am.

Pepper and Salt swap places

Pepper (*to Herr Von Cuckoo*) What is your difficulty?
Herr Von Cuckoo (*whispering*) Ich have my voice lost.
Salt (*to Pepper*) What?
Pepper (*to Salt*) Ich have my voice lost.
Salt (*to Pepper*) Well, that's very careless of you, Miss Pepper. When did you last see it?
Pepper Not *me*. Him!
Salt Ha, ha, I know. Only pulling your peppercorns! (*To Herr Von Cuckoo*) Now then, shipmate, you have lost your voice, right?
Herr Von Cuckoo Ja.
Salt Why? I will hazard a guess you have lost it on account of all that 'cuckoo, cuckoo' palaver all day long. Take my advice, have a rest. Stop 'cuckoo, cuckooing' for a few days.
Herr Von Cuckoo Impossible. Is my job.
Salt What?
Pepper Is his job. He means that a cuckoo clock that cannot 'cuckoo' is nothing short of useless. Correct?
Herr Von Cuckoo Ja.
Pepper I tend to agree. If you ask me, Mr Salt, Cuckoo could be a likely candidate for the Dustbin.

Dramatic chord

Herr Von Cuckoo Ach, nein. Nein. (*In panic, he flaps his wings*)
Salt Miss Pepper! What a cruel thing to say. Calm down, Cuckoo, calm.

Pepper I'm only being realistic. What do the Big Ones do if they've finished with something or if something doesn't work? Throw it in the Dustbin.

Herr Von Cuckoo trembles again

Bang. The end. Never seen again.

This is true. A gloomy pause

Salt He must go on leave. (*He has an idea*) To the seaside. Get some salty sea-air in your lungs and your voice'll come back loud as a fog-horn.

Pepper How do you know? You've never seen the sea. The nearest the sea *you've* ever got was that willow-pattern sauce-boat on the top shelf. And what happened to that? One day the Big Ones found it was cracked and—bang—

Salt—the Dustbin. All the more reason for Cuckoo to see the real sea. I've had salt in me all my life and I've never lost my voice. Go on, shipmate. Weigh anchor and fly away.

Her Von Cuckoo shakes his head

Why not?

Herr Von Cuckoo You forget. Ich cannot fly. My wings are wooden. (*He begins to weep with despair*)

Salt You shouldn't have mentioned the Dustbin.

Pepper thinks, then goes to comfort Herr Von Cuckoo

Pepper Herr Von Cuckoo. I was very unkind. But standing on the shelf all day I get so bored and bad-tempered. When night-time comes I take it out on my friends. I'm sorry. Forgive me.

After a pause, Herr Von Cuckoo accepts the apology, by kissing her on both cheeks

Salt Now, come on. Show a leg. All hands on deck for a party. Eh? It's after twelve-hundred hours midnight, so we're safe. We can dance and sing.

Herr Von Cuckoo points to his throat

Sorry, shipmate. You dance. We'll do the singing.

Pepper Herr Von Cuckoo, may I have the pleasure of the next waltz?

Herr Von Cuckoo cannot resist the invitation. He bows politely

Song 2 THE DRESSER HOP

This may be danced to by all three, but it would be effective if Salt could play a squeeze-box to accompany the dancing of Pepper and Herr Von Cuckoo. If considered preferable the verses may be sung in unison.

Dramatic licence suggests that Herr Von Cuckoo could join in the chorus work!

Pepper In approximately eighteen-fifty
When the dresser was new

Come midnight
The dresser-folk
Had nothing much to do

Pepper and Herr Von Cuckoo So one night they put their heads together
Came up with the answer

All And ever since ev'rybody on
The dresser's been a dancer.

So kindly take your partners
The dresser dance has begun
Come skip and hop
Round the working top
With a one, two, three, one.

Pepper As we gaily trip the light fantastic
All our cares we forget

Cuckoo Avoiding
The rolling pin
We waltz and minuet

Pepper and Salt Palais glide or military two-step
Quadrille or the Lancers

All We swing and sway till the break of day
The dresser ballroom dancers.

So kindly take your partners
The dresser dance has begun
Come skip and hop
Round the working top
With a one, two, three, one.

Salt and Pepper Herr Von Cuckoo
Dashing as a white sergeant
Jives to a gentle gavotte

Pepper No-one can fault
Mister Salt
As he saunters

Salt And at the foxtrot
Miss Pepper is hot.

All So kindly take your partners
The dresser dance has begun
Come skip and hop
Round the working top
With a one, two, three one
Come skip and hop
Round the working top
With a one, two, three,
One, two, three,
One, two, three,
One.

Salt Bravo!
Herr Von Cuckoo (*with a bow*) Danke schon.
Pepper Thank you.

Herr Von Cuckoo starts towards his clock. Pepper sighs

Salt Well, that was fun.
Pepper Old fashioned.
Salt I enjoyed it.
Pepper Only did it to cheer up Cuckoo. Oh, if only something exciting, out of the ordinary, would happen.

Suddenly Herr Von Cuckoo, who has just passed the rolling pin, flaps his wings excitedly

Herr Von Cuckoo (*croaking*) Herr Salt, Fraulein Pepper. Schnell, schnell!
Salt Smell, what smell? What's he croaking about?
Pepper Schnell. Quick.

Salt and Pepper go to the rolling pin. All look behind it

Herr Von Cuckoo Was ist das? What is zat?
Salt Let's heave-ho it over here and have a good look.

Salt and Herr Von Cuckoo pick "it" up and carry "it" over the rolling pin, standing "it" up, facing away from the audience

Funny, it's warm. (*To the audience*) Anyone seen one of these before? What is it?

The audience should shout out "a Gingerbread Man"

A what?

The audience shout again

Pepper Of course! A Gingerbread Man. The Big Ones must have baked him.
Herr Von Cuckoo Guten tag.

He goes to shake hands, but at this point, the Gingerbread Man bends at the stomach

Salt They didn't bake him very well. He's all rubbery. Hey up.

They lift the Gingerbread Man, but he collapses again. Business repeated a couple of times. His arms flail wildly. Eventually, he is still

Phew! I hope you're finished! You're heavy!
Pepper That's it! He's not!
Salt He *is*! He's very heavy.
Pepper No. Finished. He's not finished. Look. No eyes, no mouth, no nose ...
Salt No nose?
Pepper No, no nose.
Salt No no nose?
Pepper Yes!

Herr Von Cuckoo (*an idea*) Ich knows.
Salt *Your* nose?
Herr Von Cuckoo Nein. Ich *knows*. Ich idea have. Let us him finish.
Pepper How?
Herr Von Cuckoo Give him eyes und mouth und nose...
Pepper Good idea, Cuckoo; now what could we use? What could we use for eyes?

Audience participation if desired—suggestions for eyes, mouth, etc.

Currants, lemon peel—chocolate buttons?
Salt Let's find some.

They all rush to the back, in search. Slowly, the Gingerbread Man begins to topple sideways. The audience may call out. In any case, Salt suddenly sees and rushes back to catch him in time.

Salt Hey! Hup!

Salt rebalances the Gingerbread Man and returns to work. After a moment, the Gingerbread Man topples the other way. Herr Von Cuckoo has to rush in and stop him falling

Herr Von Cuckoo Ach! Ach! Ach! Hup! (*He rebalances him*)

Meanwhile various currants and peel have been collected behind the rolling pin. The Gingerbread Man begins to topple once more—towards Salt's side

Salt (*rushing back*) Hey! Come on, shipmate, on the rolling pin!

He and Herr Von Cuckoo lift him and sit him, back to audience, on the rolling pin. Tension music is heard as they "finish" the Gingerbread Man's face. This can be mimed or cheated as he is sitting back to the audience

Pepper One nose.
Herr Von Cuckoo Ein eye.
Salt Two eyes.
Pepper One mouth.
Salt Right. Reception party—assemble. I'll pipe him aboard.

Pepper and Herr Von Cuckoo stand formally. Salt blows his whistle

Salt (*to the Gingerbread Man*) Welcome aboard this dresser, shipmate.

They stand back. Salt salutes. Tension music builds—but nothing happens

Herr Von Cuckoo Is he all right?
Salt No, he's all wrong. Why won't he wake up? He's got all his tackle.
Pepper I know. Make him sneeze.
Salt How, Miss Pepper?
Pepper Me. Kindly twist my grinder a touch.

Salt obeys. Percussion accompaniment

Thank you

Pepper bends and picks up the pepper (this can be imaginary), then gingerly holds it under the Gingerbread Man's nose. Tension music. The Gingerbread Man builds to an enormous sneeze, which blows everyone back a little

Gingerbread Man A—a—a—tishoo!

The Gingerbread Man slowly starts to move, one limb at a time, until he is standing. A sudden jump turns him to face the audience for the first time. He looks excitedly about—he can see for the first time. The others come forward to watch. Suddenly he sees them and does not know how to react. Salt comes forward to shake hands

Salt Welcome aboard, shipmate. I'm Salt.
Pepper How do you do? I'm Pepper.
Herr Von Cuckoo Guten tag, mein Herr. Herr Von Cuckoo at your service. (*He bows politely*)

With an effort, the Gingerbread Man opens his mouth and tries to speak

Gingerbread Man H—ha—hall—o. Ha—llo. (*He laughs with pleasure at being able to speak*) Hallo! Salt, Pepper, Herr Von Cuckoo, hallo! (*Leaping and shouting with excitement, he jumps about, nearly knocking people over*) Hallo! Hallo! Hallo! Hallo!
Pepper Maybe I made his mouth a little large.
Salt No, no. Only the excitement of his first voyage.

The Gingerbread Man comes bounding back. He talks very loudly

Gingerbread Man I say, where am I?
Salt In the kitchen.
Pepper On the dresser.
Herr Von Cuckoo You are baked freshly.
Gingerbread Man Baked freshly?
Salt By the Big Ones.
Gingerbread Man The Big Ones?
Pepper The human people who live here.
Salt Talking of whom, I wonder, shipmate—could you turn down the volume a little? If they should wake up ...
Gingerbread Man (*just as loudly*) Certainly, Salty! Ha, ha. (*He slaps Salt on the back heartily*) Say no more.

Herr Von Cuckoo attempts to 'Shhhh' the Gingerbread Man but in vain. He leaps off to explore, moving behind a plate

Hallo! Hallo!
Herr Von Cuckoo Shhhhh!
Salt (*trying to be broadminded*) Just high spirits ...

Salt turns to see the Gingerbread Man peering behind the plate

Hey, mind that plate! Oh my.
Herr Von Cuckoo What have we done?

Pepper starts laughing

Pepper I think it's splendid!
Salt It won't be if he disturbs the Big Ones on the upper deck.
Pepper Why not? A spicy whiff of excitement. Danger. Exactly what we need. Just what I wanted.

The Gingerbread Man finds the transistor radio

Gingerbread Man (*loudly*) I say! Salty. What's this?
Salt Shhh! What?
Herr Von Cuckoo (*concerned*) Aah! Ze transistor radio.
Salt (*to Herr Von Cuckoo*) Oh no. (*To the Gingerbread Man, trying to be calm*) That, shipmate? Nothing special. I wouldn't touch it if I ...

Too late. The Gingerbread Man finds the switch and turns it on. Rock music blares out

Oh no!

The Gingerbread Man starts gyrating to the rhythm

(*Loudly*) Miss Pepper, what are we to do?

Pepper smiles at Salt gleefully and goes over to the Gingerbread Man, and starts happily gyrating with him

Mutiny! That's all we need!
Gingerbread Man (*loudly*) Hey, Pepper!
Pepper (*loudly*) Yes?
Gingerbread Man One thing nobody told me.
Pepper What?
Gingerbread Man Who *I* am?
Pepper You? You're the Gingerbread Man!

During the song, Salt and Herr Von Cuckoo eventually relent and join in

Song 3 THE GINGERBREAD MAN

Gingerbread Man Newly baked this morning
Take a look at my tan
Hey hey
I'm the Gingerbread Man
Like a magic spell I
Just appeared with a bang
Hey hey
I'm the ginger, ginger
Ginger, ginger, ginger
Ginger, ginger
Gingerbread Man.

All Ginger, ginger
Ginger, ginger, ginger

Ginger, ginger
Gingerbread Man.

Gingerbread Man Suddenly you found me
Like a flash in the pan
Hey hey
I'm the Gingerbread Man
Bold and brown and bouncy
As an orang-utan
Hey hey
I'm the ginger, ginger
Ginger, ginger, ginger
Ginger, ginger
Gingerbread man.

All Ginger, ginger
Ginger, ginger, ginger
Ginger, ginger
Gingerbread Man.

Gingerbread Man From the tips of my toes
To the top of my head
I'm guaranteed genuine
Gingerbread

All Gingerbread, gingerbread.

Salt, Pepper and Herr Von Cuckoo
Soon as you arrived the
Dresser party began
Hey hey
You're the Gingerbread Man

Pepper Ginger you're the greatest
I'm your number one fan

All Hey hey
You're the ginger, ginger
Ginger, ginger, ginger
Ginger, ginger
Gingerbread Man.

Ginger, ginger
Ginger, ginger, ginger
Ginger, ginger
Gingerbread Man.

Gingerbread Man One more time

All Ginger, ginger
Ginger, ginger, ginger
Ginger, ginger
Gingerbread Man.

At the end of the song they all applaud happily

Pepper That's more like it!
Herr Von Cuckoo Encore! Encore!
Salt I must say that was invigorating.
Gingerbread Man (*turning up the volume*) Go on then!
Salt What?
Gingerbread Man Say it!
Salt That was invigorating!

All laugh as the music starts again. They all start dancing once more

Suddenly—we hear, loudly, the noise of a door opening. Then a violent lighting change—all up to a blinding full—tells us someone has come into the kitchen

All react with horror to this. Herr Von Cuckoo scurries back to his clock, and goes inside. Pepper dashes to her original position, maybe even trying to replace the envelope. Salt has finished up near the radio, which is still blaring out. He starts to dash back to join Pepper, but suddenly remembers to turn the radio off. Then he freezes, but can see the Gingerbread Man, who has never experienced the blinding light before. He is standing transfixed

(*Whispering through clenched teeth*) Hey, Gingerbread Man. Down! Lie down!

In the nick of time, the Gingerbread Man lies down, virtually in the position he had been left. Now, as the voices of the Big Ones are heard, we see their shadows looming threateningly over the set

Mrs Big One There you are, dear, nothing.
Mr Big One Extraordinary, darling. I could have sworn I heard the radio blaring out.
Mrs Big One Well, you were wrong, dear, weren't you?
Mr Big One Must have been, I suppose.
Mrs Big One Anyway, it couldn't have just switched itself on, could it?
Mr Big One Ah, but—er—it might have been left on.
Mrs Big One What do you mean?
Mr Big One Well, darling, you er—might—not have switched it off.
Mrs Big One Of course I never switched it off—
Mr Big One Aaaah!
Mrs Big One —because *I* never switched it on in the first place. *You* did. For the football results. If anyone left it on, you did.
Mr Big One I didn't.
Mrs Big One What?
Mr Big One Leave it on.
Mrs Big One Then what are we arguing for?
Mr Big One I'm not arguing. I thought I heard music, that's all.
Mrs Big One Well, it must have come from next door. Come on, dear, I'm getting cold.
Mr Big One All right, darling. But I could have sworn I heard music.

During the last speech, the clock door opens and Herr Von Cuckoo emerges. and clears his throat (with difficulty)

Herr Von Cuckoo (*huskily*) Mi, mi, mi, mi. (*He looks up to check the time—one o'clock. Very huskily*) Cuckoo! (*He shrugs his shoulders, shakes his head and goes back inside, curled up with embarrassment*)

Mrs Big One What a weedy little noise.
Mr Big One Needs a bit of oil, maybe.
Mrs Big One Past it, more like. Have to get rid of it if it can't do better than that.

The lights return to "normal" and we hear the door slam. The shadows have gone. Pause. First to emerge is Herr Von Cuckoo. He comes out of his door, and locks it, in a terrible state

Herr Von Cuckoo Ach! Ach! Ach! Ach! "Have to get rid of it", she said. Herr Salt!

He goes towards Salt and Pepper and meets the Gingerbread Man, who is nervously shaking

Gingerbread Man Hey! What was all that about?
Herr Von Cuckoo (*avoiding the Gingerbread Man*) Bitte, Herr Salt.

Salt and Pepper move. Salt ignores Herr Von Cuckoo

Pepper (*recovering*) A-a-tishoo!
Salt (*angrily*) Gingerbread Man!
Gingerbread Man What happened?
Salt You woke up the Big Ones, that's what happened. Now listen. You're very young, the youngest member of the crew; you were only baked today. But this ship will sink if you behave ...
Pepper (*intervening*) Please, Mr Salt. Let me. Gingerbread Man. You're very welcome here; you've given us more excitement tonight than we've had for years, *but* we dresser folk, for our own good, should never cross with the Big Ones.

Herr Von Cuckoo reacts to this remark

Gingerbread Man I'm sorry.
Pepper They can be very cruel.

Herr Von Cuckoo starts sobbing

Salt Cheer up, Cuckoo.
Herr Von Cuckoo Did not you hear? Zey will throw me in the Dustbin.
Gingerbread Man What's the Dustbin?
Pepper Anything they don't want, the Big Ones throw in the Dustbin and it's never seen again.

Herr Von Cuckoo sobs even more

Sorry, Cuckoo, but he must be told.
Gingerbread Man Why should they want to throw Cuckoo away?

Herr Von Cuckoo sobs even more

Herr Von Cuckoo Because ich have a toad in ze throat.
Salt I think you mean 'frog', shipmate.
Herr Von Cuckoo Frog, toad, what is ze difference?
Salt Well, a toad is larger with fatter cheeks ...

Herr Von Cuckoo sobs again

I'm sorry, shipmate. Most unfeeling.
Pepper The point is, he can't sing his cuckoos; he's a cuckoo-less cuckoo clock cuckoo.

Herr Von Cuckoo sobs harder

Gingerbread Man Listen. Let me help. To make up for waking the Big Ones.
Herr Von Cuckoo What could *you* do?
Gingerbread Man Find something to make you better.
Pepper Something to soothe a sore throat.
Salt What have we got on board that's soothing? Silky smooth, full of goodness?

Hopefully the audience will help by shouting out "honey". This will work if the pot (on the shelf) is marked clearly enough to have been established

Pepper Of course, honey!
Gingerbread Man Honey. Right, where is it?
Salt It means a voyage of exploration to the High Shelf.

Dramatic chord. All look up at the honey

Gingerbread Man Simple! Back in a jiffy.

The Gingerbread Man walks towards the back. The others look at each other

Salt Wait!

The Gingerbread Man turns

Before you set sail ...
Pepper Beware.
Gingerbread Man Beware?
Herr Von Cuckoo Of ze Old Bag.
Gingerbread Man Of what?
All Three The Old Bag.
Pepper The most horrible, dangerous, ruthless—tea-bag.
Salt The terror of the High Shelf.

Song 4 BEWARE OF THE OLD BAG

If considered preferable the verses may be sung in unison

Pepper She lives in the teapot up there
Salt But to visit her—don't you dare
Herr Von Cuckoo She keeps herself
To her shelf
Salt And her shelf
To herself
All And trespassers had better...
Beware
Of the Old Bag
She's not fond of company
Take care
She's an old hag
She's nobody's cup of tea.

Pepper She's the terror of the teapot
And her temper's quick to brew
Salt From the gloom she will loom
Like a ghost to frighten you
Salt So look out,
Pepper Look out,
Herr Von Cuckoo Look out,
All She's lying in wait
Ev'ry perforation oozing hate.
Beware
Of the Old Bag
She's not fond of company
Take care
She's an old hag
She's nobody's cup of tea.

Salt And she hides behind the herb jars
Looking out for passing spies
Pepper If you peep, out she'll creep
Herr Von Cuckoo And you'll get a big surprise
All So look out, look out, look out
For Gingerbread Man
She will surely catch you if she can.

Beware
Of the Old Bag
She's not fond of company
Take care

She's an old hag
She's nobody's cup of tea.

Herr Von Cuckoo So look out,
Pepper Look out,
Salt Look out,
All Take care
Beware.

Towards the end of the song, the Gingerbread Man has been 'frightened' by the others to hide behind the rolling pin. Now, at the end of the song, as the others freeze in their final positions, arms outspread for the big finish, we hear a ghostly noise

Gingerbread Man (*behind the rolling pin*) Woooooh, Woooooooooh!

Dramatic rumble. The others face front and react frightened, as a ghostly figure looms from behind the rolling pin. It is the Gingerbread Man with a tea cloth over his head

Salt
Pepper
Herr Von Cuckoo } (*in a frightened whisper*) The Old Bag! { *Speaking together*

The Gingerbread Man creeps to one side, making his ghostly noise. The others tremble with fear. All together they turn their eyes to the noise, see the apparition, react, turn, bump into each other, and then, all together, run screaming to the side edge of the dresser. Gingerbread Man pursues. They, having apparently nearly fallen off the dresser, run in their group to the other side. He pursues them to the edge. They nearly "fall off", then in their huddle escape to the centre. The Gingerbread Man throws the tea cloth over them. They punch around inside it, and then emerge from it. The Gingerbread Man is laughing

Pepper It was him all the time. (*She sneezes to recover*)
Gingerbread Man (*laughing*) Sorry, Pepper. Just a little joke.
Salt Just a little joke? We nearly fell overboard, didn't we Cuckoo?
Herr Von Cuckoo opens his mouth to reply, but nothing comes out
Eh?

Herr Von Cuckoo tries again. Now all take notice. Not a sound comes out. He shakes his head

(*To the others*) Listen.
Gingerbread Man I can't hear anything.
Salt Exactly. There's nothing to hear. Cuckoo's got no voice at all. Come on, shipmate, I'll take you home.

Music, as the sad Cuckoo is led by Salt to his door. As they go in, Pepper and Gingerbread Man, who have watched in a sort of worried reverie, snap out of it

Pepper The honey. Please. You'll have to hurry. It's an emergency now.
Gingerbread Man Certainly, certainly, quick as I can. You can rely on the Gingerbread Man!

Music, as he flexes himself in preparation. Pepper watches as he advances to the shelf. He jumps to reach it, but cannot (or reaches it but cannot pull himself up). He tries this a couple of times, unsuccessfully, then looks at Pepper in consternation. She looks around

Pepper Sugar lumps!

Pepper runs to the sugar bowl. She and the Gingerbread Man take out three or four lumps and make a pile, leaving a "step" on each one. Gingerly the Gingerbread Man climbs the pile, but at the last minute he topples over and the pile collapses. He lands on the "floor". At this moment, Salt emerges from the cuckoo clock

Salt Ahoy there! What's up?
Gingerbread Man I'm down! (*Setting up the sugar lumps again*) Just on my way.
Salt You'll never get up there like that.
Pepper Think of a better way.
Salt Well ... Well ... Well ...

As Salt thinks, the Gingerbread Man again climbs the sugar lumps, topples and falls again. He makes an angry frustrated noise

Pepper Well?
Salt Well ...
Pepper Come on. Here's a chance to show off your nautical know-how.
Salt I'm thinking, I'm thinking. What would a real old salt of the sea do? Got it! A capstan.
Gingerbread Man Of course! A capstan! (*Pause*) What's a capstan?
Salt I'll show you, shipmate. Miss Pepper, be good enough to heave-ho that piece of string that came on the Big Ones' parcel yesterday.
Pepper String. (*She goes to find it, stops and turns, and smiles*) Aye, aye, Captain! (*She salutes and carries on. She is thoroughly enjoying the excitement*)
Salt Gingerbread Man. Give us a hand rolling the rolling pin.
Gingerbread Man Aye, aye, Captain.

Salt and the Gingerbread Man push the rolling pin to beneath the shelf, under a vacant cup hook on the shelf edge above their heads

Pepper (*returning*) String, Captain.
Salt Splendid. Thank you, Miss Pepper. Now, everybody, I'll show you the Captain's Capstan!

Music—shanty-style, the intro to Song 5, as Salt, helped by the other two, prepares the capstan. First he throws the string over the cup hook, above. Then he gives one end to the Gingerbread Man, showing him how to tie it round his waist as a kind of sling-hoist. (The slip-knot could already be there.) The other end of the string is tied round the thick part of the rolling pin, which should be up stage. The string should be taut. Then Salt and Pepper roll the rolling pin forwards (downstage), having the effect of lifting the Gingerbread Man off the ground. He will probably have to help himself, by using the side of the dresser, and finally helping himself climb onto the shelf

Song 5 HEAVE-HO, A-ROLLING GO

Salt Haul on the halyard, hard as we can
All Heave-ho, a-rolling go
Salt Hup, mates, and hoist the Gingerbread Man
All Way hay and yo ho ho.

Salt Lifting our load and taking the strain
All Heave-ho, a-rolling go
Salt Turning the capstan, cranking the crane
All Way hay and yo ho ho.

Salt Higher and higher, t'ward the crow's nest
All Heave-ho, a-rolling go
Salt Fair wind and fortune follow the quest
All Way hay and yo ho ho.

The Music continues as the Gingerbread Man removes the loop of string and hangs it from the hook, and waves down to Salt and Pepper, who then sit and wait on the rolling pin. Lighting changes to the shelf area only. Tension music as the Gingerbread Man sets off towards the honey, treading on tiptoe

Suddenly the door of the cottage teapot creaks menacingly open, and the Old Bag peeps out, then seeing the invader of "her" territory, surreptitiously creeps out and starts stalking the Gingerbread Man

The audience will pretty certainly react, by shouting a warning to the Gingerbread Man, who by this time has reached the honey and is starting to remove the lid. The Old Bag, looming like a ghost, advances and the Gingerbread Man senses danger; he mimes to the audience "Is there someone behind me?"; "Yes", comes back the reply. He works himself up to a sudden quick turn; but the Old Bag has been too quick for him, and hidden behind other jars and bottles. The Gingerbread Man assumes the audience is leading him up the garden path, and returns to the honey jar. The business is repeated as the Old Bag creeps out and advances again. This time, encouraged by the audience, he turns suddenly, and sees the Old Bag—surprising her at the same time. Both scream and run to hide in opposite directions. They re-emerge and go into a panto-style stalking—the Gingerbread Man never seeing the Old Bag and vice versa—back to back, until they bump into each other, jump violently, and confront one another

Old Bag (*sharply*) Who are you?
Gingerbread Man The G-G-G-Gingerbread Man.
Old Bag Never heard of you.
Gingerbread Man I was only b-b-baked today. By the Big Ones.
Old Bag You're trespassing.
Gingerbread Man But ...
Old Bag This is *my* shelf.
Gingerbread Man But this is an emergency. Herr Von Cuckoo ...
Old Bag What about him?

Gingerbread Man He's lost his voice.
Old Bag You mean he can't "cuckoo"?
Gingerbread Man Yes. I mean no.
Old Bag (*with a sudden cackle*) Ha, ha, ha.
Gingerbread Man So I thought ...
Old Bag (*with a sudden change back to sharpness*) What did you think?
Gingerbread Man I thought I'd get him some honey. It might help him.
Old Bag You thought wrong.
Gingerbread Man You mean honey won't help him?
Old Bag I mean you're not getting him any. I'm glad, delighted he's lost his voice. I've always hated that stupid noise every hour of the day and night. "Cuckoo, Cuckoo, Cuckoo." Now perhaps I can get a bit of peace and quiet.
Gingerbread Man But the Big Ones may throw him in the Dustbin.
Old Bag Good riddance. And good riddance to you, too. Clear off. (*To the audience*) And *you* can clear off too. All of you.
Gingerbread Man What have *they* done?
Old Bag They don't like me.
Gingerbread Man How do you know?
Old Bag Nobody likes me. I'm all alone. All the other tea bags in my packet were used up ages ago. The Big Ones missed me and I hid in the tea pot. No-one ever visits me.
Gingerbread Man Well, it's not easy getting here.
Old Bag It's not easy *living* here.
Gingerbread Man Are you lonely?
Old Bag I never said that.
Gingerbread Man I'll be your friend, if you like.
Old Bag Huh. Bribery. Get round me. Let's be friends. Then I give you the honey. Whoosh, down. Never see you again.
Gingerbread Man No! We'll all be your friends. (*Encouraging the audience to shout "Yes"*) Won't we?
Old Bag Don't believe it.
Gingerbread Man Why not?
Old Bag People have to like you to be friends with you. And they don't like me. I'll prove it. Hands up all those who don't like tea. Mm? All those who prefer tasteless, rubbishy drinks like orange or cherryade or lemon squash.

The aim is to get all the children in the audience to put up their hands

There you are! Hardly anyone likes tea. Look at those little hands of hatred!
Gingerbread Man Some of the older ones like you.
Old Bag But how many of them like whisky or gin or beer or even coffee more than they like *me*? Eh? Come on. Hands up!

The aim is to get at least some of the adults to raise their hands

There you are. Nobody likes me!
Gingerbread Man I don't think you like them very much!

Old Bag I never said that. I'm quite enjoying a bit of company.
Gingerbread Man Good (*Indicating the honey*) Then will you let me take some ...
Old Bag (*interrupting*) I'll tell your fortune for you, if you like.
Gingerbread Man Will you? How?
Old Bag Tea leaves have always had special magic fortune-telling properties. They send messages through my perforations. Show me your hand.
Gingerbread Man Well ...

The Gingerbread Man tentatively stretches out his hand

Old Bag Come along. Don't be shy.

Song 6 THE POWER OF THE LEAF

Old Bag
If you want to know the future
You don't need a horoscope
You don't need to study stars
Through a telescope
You don't need a pack of tarot cards
You don't need a crystal ball
For the power of the tea leaf
Is more potent than them all.

So
Put your belief
In the power of the leaf
It can tell you things you never knew before
Put your belief
In the power of the leaf
If you want to know what lies in store.

No, there isn't any secret,
There's no club you have to join
And you needn't cross my palm
With a silver coin
You don't need to say a magic word
You don't need a medium
Through the power of the tea leaf
See the shape of things to come.

So
Put your belief
Gingerbread Man (*spoken echo*) Put your belief
Old Bag In the power of the leaf
Gingerbread Man (*spoken echo*) In the power of the leaf
Old Bag It can tell you things you never knew before
Both Put your belief
In the power of the leaf
If you want to know what lies in store.

The music continues

Gingerbread Man (*speaking*) What can you see?
Old Bag A message.
Gingerbread Man For me?
Old Bag Yes. Listen and learn.
"When trouble comes, if you can cope,
Three lives will shortly find new hope."
Gingerbread Man "When trouble comes, if I can cope,
Three lives will shortly find new hope."
What does it mean?
Old Bag You'll find out—soon.
Gingerbread Man Thank you, Old Bag.
Old Bag Don't thank me, thank the power of the leaf.

Old Bag *and* **Gingerbread Man** (*singing*)

So
Put your belief
In the power of the leaf
It can tell you things you never knew before
Put your belief
In the power of the leaf
If you want to know what lies in store.

Put your belief
In the power of the leaf
It can tell you things you never knew before
Put your belief
In the power of the leaf
If you want to know what lies in store.

Old Bag Don't forget.
Gingerbread Man Thank you, Old Bag. Well, it's time for me to go down again.
Old Bag (*sharply*) Why? Don't you enjoy my company?
Gingerbread Man Yes, but the others are ...
Old Bag (*charmingly*) Let me show you round my shelf. (*She grabs him by an arm, and leads him across*) See my herb garden? Sage, rosemary, thyme, marjoram ...
Gingerbread Man What are they for?
Old Bag They contain remarkable medicinal powers. I have studied them hard and long. They can cure diseases, make sick folk better.
Gingerbread Man Nobody told me you could do that.
Old Bag Nobody else knows.
Gingerbread Man But think of the good you could do for the dresser folk. The help you could be.
Old Bag Nobody's ever asked for my help.
Gingerbread Man I'm asking you now. To help Cuckoo.
Old Bag That noisy bird?

Gingerbread Man Just a small lump of honey ...
Old Bag No, no, no! I must be getting senile. Soft. I was beginning to like you. But you weren't being friendly at all.
Gingerbread I was!
Old Bag All you want is your rotten honey. And if I give you some I'll never see you again.
Gingerbread Man You will.
Old Bag Clear off.
Gingerbread Man I'll come back.
Old Bag (*shouting*) Get off my shelf.

Furious, the Old Bag stomps back to the teapot and goes inside

Music, as the Gingerbread Man considers what to do. He looks at the honey, then at the place of descent, perhaps checking for confirmation with the audience. He makes his mind up, and, having checked that the teapot door is still closed, he tiptoes to the honey jar and steals a chunk. He checks once more that the coast is clear, then creeps to where he left his string harness. He looks over the edge

Gingerbread Man (*whispering*) Salty. Pepper. Psssst. Salty.

Salt and Pepper are dozing on the rolling pin. Salt stirs and wakes up. The lighting changes to reveal below

Psssst.
Pepper (*waking*) A-a-a-tishoo!
Salt What? What?
Gingerbread Man (*whispering*) Up here!
Salt (*looking up; loudly*) It's Gingerbread Man!
Gingerbread Man Shhhhh!
Music. The Gingerbread Man shows Salt the honey, and mimes throwing it down. Salt understands, wakes up Pepper, hushing her and pointing up to the Gingerbread Man.
They whisper briefly, then go to the back and bring forward a plate. Meanwhile, the Gingerbread Man looks anxiously back at the teapot door. Salt and Pepper hold the plate underneath, and the Gingerbread Man prepares to throw down the honey. At this point the teapot door creaks open. The audience will probably shout a warning, as a result of which the Gingerbread Man throws the honey down on to the plate, and desperately puts on the string harness. Meanwhile, below, Salt and Pepper place the plate down, out of the way, and return to the "capstan" rolling pin. With a cry of "anchors away", they lower him to their level

During this, the Old Bag emerges, shouting abuse. She reaches the edge of the shelf just too late

Old Bag You double-crossing little thief! I saw you! Let me get my hands on you! I'll make you squirm! Stealing deserves punishment and punished you will be! You evil little trickster. Come back.

By this time the Gingerbread Man has reached the floor and Salt and Pepper help him off with the string harness. During the next speech the Gingerbread Man becomes subdued. Music to heighten the situation

(*with a deliberately nasty change of tack*) You won't get away with it, you know. Gingerbread Man. Can you hear me? You'll soon suffer. You won't be around much longer. The Big Ones bake Gingerbread Men—to eat them. While they're fresh and crisp and tasty. Eat them. Good-bye Gingerbread Man. Good-bye for ever.

Laughing, the Old Bag backs away and returns inside the teapot

The Gingerbread Man, stunned by her words, is led to the rolling pin by Salt and Pepper; they sit him down

Gingerbread Man Is it true?
Salt Well, shipmate, we can't say for certain ...
Pepper But—well, normally, if the Big Ones bake anything ...
Gingerbread Man I see.
Salt Sorry, shipmate.
Pepper We didn't say anything because—well, you seemed so happy. And you cheered all of us up.
Salt *And* you were brave enough to answer Cuckoo's S.O.S.
Gingerbread Man Cuckoo! (*He jumps up*) I must tell him we've got his honey. (*He sets off, then stops and looks back*) And don't worry about me! (*He smiles*) I'm not beaten—till I'm eaten! And I won't be eaten—till I'm beaten!

Music as the Gingerbread Man leaves Salt and Pepper to relax on the rolling pin, and crosses to the cuckoo clock, on the way possibly placing the plate in a central position. He reaches the clock and knocks on the door

Herr Von Cuckoo!

The door opens. The sickly Herr Von Cuckoo emerges. He starts to speak

Don't speak! Save your voice! Just to let you know I fetched some honey. For your throat.

Herr Von Cuckoo takes in the news, then grabs the startled Gingerbread Man and kisses him on both cheeks, making husky noises meaning "Danke, danke!"

Gingerbread Man My pleasure, Cuckoo. It's over there, on a plate. Coming now?

Herr Von Cuckoo shakes his head and points to the clock face, which says ten to two. Then he mimes "cuckoo, cuckoo"

You've got to do some "cuckooing" first?

Herr Von Cuckoo nods

Can't you give it a miss this once? You're not well.

Herr Von Cuckoo shakes his head effusively. He must do his duty

All right. But you'll try the honey afterwards?

Herr Von Cuckoo nods and grunts, "Ja, danke"

Fine. Your throat is sore, you're feeling sick—
A dose of honey will do the trick!

Herr Von Cuckoo goes back into the clock. Music as the Gingerbread Man leaves, and returns to Salt and Pepper, on the rolling pin. He yawns, and sits on the floor, against the rolling pin, as if to go to sleep.

Gingerbread Man Goodnight

Salt and Pepper Goodnight

The Gingerbread Man begins to drop off to sleep. Suddenly there is a loud noise, scratching and scuffling. The Gingerbread Man jumps awake and listens. The noise stops. He settles again. The noise starts again. He listens again. He decides to investigate. Meanwhile Salt and Pepper have gone to sleep.

The Gingerbread Man halts in his tracks. The noise stops. He takes a couple of steps. The noise starts again. He listens. It stops. Two steps. It starts again. The Gingerbread man tracks down the noise to behind a plate, which stands vertical in the corner of the back of the dresser. Inquisitive, he tentatively slides the plate to one side. A hole is revealed in the back of the dresser.

Sleek the Mouse enters, sniffing hungrily, at the same time looking around to make sure the coast is clear

The Gingerbread Man watches, half hidden behind the plate

Sleek (*to nobody in particular*) O guys you K—I mean, O.K. you guys. This is a raid. One move and you'll feel my false teeth—no, I mean, one false move and you'll feel my teeth.

Song 7 SLEEK THE MOUSE

N.B. To prick the balloon of Sleek's cool exterior, the song should be staged in such a way that little things suddenly frighten him or go wrong—then he has to work hard to cover his embarrassment and preserve his image

Sleek the Mouse You hear scratching
In the skirting
In the kitchen
Of your house—
Then it's odds on
That you're list'ning
To yours truly—
Sleek the Mouse.

I mean bus'ness
No-one bugs me
I'm not playing
Hide and squeak
Double-cross me
At your peril
I'm the boss mouse—
Call me Sleek.

I went raiding
In the pantry
In the middle
Of the night
When the Big Ones
Caught me nibbling
Pink blancmange
They got a fright.

Tried to catch me
In a mouse trap
But I fooled them
With such ease
And next morning
Trap was empty
No-one told them—
I hate cheese!

Any showdown
I can handle
With a human,
Mouse or cat
And my whiskers
Start to tremble
If you call me—
(A) dirty rat!

I'm a hungry
Desperado
So I'm forced to
Use my nouse
That comes easy
To the ruthless
One and only
Mafia mouse.

Super-mouse
Call me Sleek
Sleek the Mouse
Pretty chic

Sleek!

He goes to lean nonchalantly in a final position, against the mug—but misses it and falls to the ground

Sleek gets up and sniffs hungrily again

Somewhere I snack a sniff—sniff a snack. A lip-smackin', paw-lickin', whisker-itchin', nose-twitchin', supersnack. And I'm gonna track it down. For days my belly's been empty and I've had a bellyful! (*He sniffs*)

The Gingerbread Man emerges. Not suspecting danger, he approaches and stands by Sleek during the following

I'm gonna nose my follow and nothing's gonna stand in my way ... (*He turns and bumps into the Gingerbread Man*) Aaaaaah!

Gingerbread Man Hallo.
Sleek You're standing in my way, stranger.
Gingerbread Man I'm the Gingerbread Man.

He shakes hands with Sleek

Sleek Hi, Ginger. I'm Sleek the Mouse. And I'm telling you this dresser ain't big enough for both of us.
Gingerbread Man I don't know what you mean.

Sleek sniffs, realizes the scent is near, sniffs his hand which was shaken by the Gingerbread Man's—and realizes

Sleek Hey. It's you! You're my little snackeroo!
Gingerbread Man What?
Sleek You smell good enough to eat, Ginger.
Gingerbread Man (*realizing the threat*) I *am*, (*suddenly*) but not by you!

Music, as a chase starts

The Gingerbread Man escapes through Sleek's legs, possibly making him fall over. The Gingerbread Man runs back to the plate and hides behind it. Sleek follows, and goes behind the plate. As he does so, the Gingerbread Man emerges from the other side of the plate and runs round it. Sleek follows. The chase round is repeated

The Gingerbread Man emerges, and stops, then gingerly backs towards the other side of the plate. Suddenly Sleek comes out from that other side, having tricked the Gingerbread Man by not going the full circuit. He pounces. The Gingerbread Man manages to struggle free, but is forced to back away to the edge of the dresser. Sleek pounces again, but the Gingerbread Man slips sideways out of the way, leaving Sleek perilously near falling off. He teeters and totters alarmingly. Meanwhile, the Gingerbread Man dashes back to the rolling pin and wakes up Salt and Pepper, who react animatedly to the situation. They quickly decide that the Gingerbread Man should go aloft to the shelf. So Salt helps him up, winding the capstan

Meanwhile, Sleek recovers his balance and turns to be faced by Pepper. They size each other up, then Pepper twists her grinder, picks up some pepper and throws it towards Sleek, who sneezes violently, but half-heartedly carries on the chase, which continues in the rolling pin area, involving Salt too. Up on the shelf, Gingerbread Man, supposedly out of harm's way, watches and shouts encouragement

Suddenly the teapot door opens, and a furious Old Bag pops out, screaming vengeance

The Gingerbread Man senses her approach and a mini-chase starts
Everyone is in motion on both levels when we hear, as before, the loud noise of the door opening. Then the violent lighting change up to a blinding full. All except Sleek pause frozen for a second, realize what has happened and dash to their normal positions. The Old Bag returns in the teapot, Salt and Pepper to their spot, and the Gingerbread Man, not being able to climb down in time, lies flat on the shelf. Sleek, unaware of what has happened, stands transfixed and wide-eyed. Then we hear the voices of the Big Ones

Mrs Big One There was no need for you to come down, dear.
Mr Big One But you said you heard noises, darling.
Mrs Big One I did, dear, funny scuffling noi ... Aaaaaaah! Look.
Mr Big One Heavens. A mouse!
Mrs Big One (*screaming*) Aaaaaaah!
Mr Big One Shoo, shoo, you verminous little rodent. Shoo, shoo.

The "Aaaaaaahs" and the "Shoo shoos" continue ad-lib, until Sleek comes to his senses, and scurries to shelter—towards his hole behind the plate

He's gone, darling.
Mrs Big One He hasn't, he's hiding! Ughhh!
Mr Big One All right, darling. I'll put some poison down.

We hear noises of, say, a cupboard door and a tin opening

Here you are, you wretched rodent. This'll teach you. Poison. One gulp and you're a gonna.

Music, as from above the stage floats down some poison (glitter?) on to the plate on which the honey waits for Cuckoo

Mrs Big One Thank you, dear.
Mr Big One Come on, darling, let's go back to bed.

At this moment Herr Von Cuckoo slowly and painfully comes out of his clock. It is two o'clock. He sadly croaks

Herr Von Cuckoo Cuckoo, cuckoo. (*Hardly any noise comes out. He shakes his head*)
Mr Big One Huh. That cuckoo's no better. Hopeless.
Mrs Big One I'll deal with it in the morning, dear.

The door slams shut, and the bright light goes out. Everybody except Herr Von Cuckoo remains frozen after all the panic. Herr Von Cuckoo, reacting to the last words of the Big Ones, looks over to the plate, and smiles

Herr Von Cuckoo (*huskily*) Herr Von Cuckoo will show you. In ze morning, thanks to ze Gingerbread Man's honey, ich will quite better be! (*Happily,* *he leaves the clock, arrives on the dresser and starts walking towards the poisoned plate of honey. He was in his clock when the Big Ones put down the poison, and therefore has no idea there is any danger.)*

The audience, hopefully, scream a warning, and as he reaches the plate and prepares to eat—

The CURTAIN *falls*

ACT II

Act II begins where Act I ended. It is suggested, to avoid the possibility of the audience missing the vital first few minutes of this act (because of late return to seats, taking time to settle etc.) that an entr'acte be played, after *the houselights go down and* before *the* CURTAIN *rises*

The CURTAIN *rises. A smiling Herr Von Cuckoo rubs his hands in anticipation, bends down—and eats some of the poisoned honey. The audience may shout out another warning. The Gingerbread Man, still flat out following the Big Ones' visit, opens his eyes and sees Herr Von Cuckoo eat just too late. He shouts down to him*

Gingerbread Man Cuckoo!
Herr Von Cuckoo Mein friend. How can ich danke you? Ich better already feel!

He goes to take more. The Gingerbread Man stops him, shouting

Gingerbread Man No!

Salt and Pepper bustle across and pull away the plate. Then Salt helps the Gingerbread Man down, using the string

Salt Did he eat any?
Gingerbread Man One mouthful.
Herr Von Cuckoo Was is ze matter? You honey fetchen me, zen away taken.
Pepper It was poisoned, Cuckoo. Poisoned by the Big Ones.
Herr Von Cuckoo (*disbelieving*) Nein. (*He laughs*) You make ze bit of a joke with me, hah? Listen. (*He happily shows how improved his voice is*) Cuckoo! Cuckoo! Cuckoo. (*But after a couple of smiling "Cuckoos", he clutches his stomach and sways. He goes on cuckooing, but it becomes more and more painful, until finally he faints backwards into the arms of Salt and the Gingerbread Man.*)

Pepper Quick, lie him down.
Salt Aye, aye ma'am.
Pepper Where's the tea cloth?
Salt Behind the rolling pin.

Pepper fetches the tea cloth and covers Herr Von Cuckoo to keep him warm

Gingerbread Man What are we going to do?

Salt listens to Herr Von Cuckoo's heart

Pepper Nothing much we *can* do. Just wait and hope he didn't eat too much.
Salt He's still breathing. Just. If only we had a ship's doctor.

Pause

Gingerbread Man But we have!
Salt What?
Gingerbread Man Well, not a doctor exactly, but she could help.
Pepper Who?
Gingerbread Man The Old Bag. With her herbs. "They can cure diseases, make sick folk better", she said.
Salt She won't come to the rescue. Never has before. Remember that jelly mould, Miss Pepper?
Pepper Yes. Top shelf she was. In the shape of a rabbit.
Salt She was made of metal—one day she started getting rusty.
Pepper Next day. Bang. The Dustbin.
Salt The Old Bag never lifted a leaf to help.
Gingerbread Man Did anyone ask her to help?
Pepper Huh. No-one dared to go near her.
Salt Waste of time, anyway.
Gingerbread Man If you didn't ask her, you could hardly expect her to help. (*He turns and looks up to the shelf, and the teapot*) Hey! Old Bag. Can you hear me? (*Pause.*) Old Bag! We need your help. Please.

No response

Salt It's no use, shipmate.

Herr Von Cuckoo groans with pain. The Gingerbread Man hears; it makes up his mind for him. He goes to the string hoist and starts putting it on

What are you doing?
Gingerbread Man Come on. Hoist me up again. The Old Bag is Cuckoo's only chance.
Salt But ...
Pepper He's right, Mr Salt. Let him try.
Gingerbread Man Quick.
Salt (*after a pause*) Aye, aye sir!

Salt and Pepper man the rolling pin capstan

Song 7A: HEAVE-HO, A-ROLLING GO (reprise)

Salt Haul on the halyard, hard as we can
All Heave-ho, a-rolling go
Salt Hup, mates, and hoist the Gingerbread Man
All Way hay and yo ho ho.

Gingerbread Man S.O.S.—urgent! I'll do my best,
All Heave-ho, a-rolling go
Salt Fair wind and fortune follow your quest
All Way hay and yo ho ho.

The Gingerbread Man arrives on the shelf. Below, Salt and Pepper sit on the rolling pin, looking at the prostrate Cuckoo. The lighting intensifies on the shelf as the Gingerbread Man takes off his string hoist and leaves it on the cup-hook. Music continues as he approaches the teapot. He is determined, though not over-confident. He knocks on the door, turning away from it as he waits for a reply. Nothing. He knocks again, and again turns away. No response at first, but then silently the door opens. The Gingerbread Man is unaware of this

The Old Bag slowly emerges

The Gingerbread Man goes to knock on the door again, but in fact knocks the Old Bag on the nose

Old Bag Ow!

The Gingerbread Man jumps with surprise

Gingerbread Man Ooh!
Old Bag (*furious*) First you pinch my honey, now you knock me on the nose.
Gingerbread Man I'm sorry. I didn't hear you ...
Old Bag Clear off!
Gingerbread Man No, please.
Old Bag Clear off! And if you ever come on my shelf again, I'll...
Gingerbread Man (*shouting*) I need your help.

Pause

Old Bag What?
Gingerbread Man (*sincerely*) I need your help.
Old Bag (*softening*) What for?
Gingerbread Man It's Cuckoo.
Old Bag That noisy bird again? I helped him when you helped yourself to my honey.
Gingerbread Man He's been poisoned—
Old Bag (*losing her temper*) How dare you? My honey is pure and health-giving ...
Gingerbread Man —by the Big Ones.
Old Bag The Big Ones? Why?
Gingerbread Man They put poison on his honey—

The Old Bag looks indignant for a second

—I mean *your* honey. Look.

He leads the Old Bag to the edge of the shelf and shows her the sight of the prostrate Herr Von Cuckoo below

Old Bag But why?
Gingerbread Man They wanted to get rid of Sleek the Mouse.

At the mention of the Mouse, the Old Bag becomes nervous

Old Bag Mouse? What mouse?
Gingerbread Man Sleek. The mouse that's trying to eat me.

Old Bag Eat you? Where? Has he followed you? (*She looks around, wild-eyed*)
Gingerbread Man No. Probably went home when he saw the poison pouring down.
Old Bag I hate mice. Vicious creatures. They try to chew my perforations.

Suddenly, from a hole behind the herb jars, if necessary pushing between them, comes Sleek the Mouse

Sleek O.K. Ginger, don't move. Show for a timedown—time for a show-down.
Old Bag Aaaaah. A mouse! Help! Help! (*She gathers in her perforations in terror*).
Gingerbread Man Shhhh! Go away, Sleek. I'm not frightened of you. (*He does not sound convincing*)

Meanwhile Salt and Pepper have heard the Old Bag's screams and stand below, looking at the scene above

Sleek No? Reckoned you were safe up here, huh? Reckoned I couldn't climb dressers too? Think again, Ginger. I used the back entrance.
Old Bag (*wailing*) Get rid of him!

Sleek cannot see the Old Bag behind the Gingerbread Man

Sleek You've had your fun, Ginger. Now it's my turn. I'm starving.
Gingerbread Man You may be hungry, but try as you can, you'll never eat the Gingerbread Man.

Music. Sleek the Mouse and the Gingerbread Man move towards each other "High Noon" style. Left on her own, the Old Bag trembles by the edge of the shelf. Sleek and the Gingerbread Man circle each other. Then, say, three times Sleek lunges at the Gingerbread Man, who steps aside to avoid him. Then they clasp hands in a trial of strength. Slowly but surely Sleek gains supremacy till the Gingerbread Man is down. Then Sleek sniffs hungrily at the Gingerbread Man's arm, and prepares to bite it. He has his back to the Old Bag. Very bravely, seeing the situation, the Old Bag, who has started to creep home to her teapot, decides she should help the Gingerbread Man. She looms up on Sleek, and pulls his tail

Sleek Aah!

In this second or two of panic, the Gingerbread Man rolls away from Sleek's grasp and dashes to the hole behind the herb jars. He disappears

Sleek (*realizing what has happened*) You miserable Old Bag. You'll pay for that.

Music continues as they stalk each other. Finally the Old Bag is backed towards the edge of the shelf. The Gingerbread Man arrives below (through the mouse hole behind the plate). He rushes to Salt and Pepper, who have been watching. They consult in a huddle, then grab the tea cloth off the prostrate Herr Von

Cuckoo, and hold it under the shelf (firemen's blanket-style). Alternatively the others position the upturned mug for her to step down on. The tension builds as Sleek advances and finally the Old Bag jumps or falls from the shelf into the tea cloth. She is taken care of, as the lights focus on the furious Sleek above. During his next speech, the Gingerbread Man, taking the tea cloth with him, goes back through the hole behind the plate

I've been boozlebammed!Bamboozled! You dirty, stinking rats! (*Petulantly whining*) There were two of you against one of me. (*He suddenly cries with frustration and injustice, the aim being to get the audience to laugh at him*) It's not fair! Boo hoo hoo hoo! (*He hears the audience laughing at him and looks up, furious*) Hey! It's not funny. Nobody laughs at me, O.K.? I'm the baddie. The tough guy. A savage brute. And I'm telling you—(*he crumples again*)—it wasn't fair! Boo hoo hoo!

Hopefully the audience are laughing again

Shut up! I'm warning you. I'm a mouseless ruth—ruthless mouse—(*he has an idea*)—and I'm so hungry that one more squeak from you and I'll be down there—raiding your sweets. All those toffees, and sherbet lemons and chocolate eclairs ... (*He laughs and sniffs greedily. His sniffs suddenly change as he realizes he can detect something tasty nearby*)

Through the hole, carrying the tea cloth, the Gingerbread Man appears

Gingerbread Man Coo—ee!

Music, as Sleek sees the Gingerbread Man and prepares to attack. He charges a few times, warded off by the Gingerbread Man, who uses the tea cloth like a bullfighter's cape—with appropriate music. Finally the Gingerbread Man manoeuvres himself to the tea pot, the door of which is still open. With a final flourish he makes Sleek charge him and steps aside, forcing Sleek to run into the tea pot. Swiftly, the Gingerbread Man slams the door shut, and either locks it or places something against it to stop it opening. The others below have been watching, and now applaud. The Gingerbread Man bows graciously and throws down the tea cloth to be put back on Herr Von Cuckoo. Pepper returns to tend Herr Von Cuckoo

Thank you, thank you. (*Looking over the edge*) All right, Old Bag?

Old Bag No. You've shut him in my teapot. (*Wailing*) There's a mouse in my house!

Gingerbread Man Oh, sorry. I'll let him out, shall I?

Old Bag What?

Gingerbread Man Let him come down and nibble your perforations.

Old Bag No, no. Leave him.

Gingerbread Man Some folk are never satisfied. (*He sits on the edge*)

Old Bag I am, I am. Thankyou. Thank you *all* for saving me.

Salt (*uncomfortably*) Our duty ma'am. Anyone in danger on the High Shelf...

Old Bag But you'd rather it hadn't been me, eh?

Salt No, but...

Old Bag You don't like me, do you?
Salt I ...
Old Bag You think I'm a miserable Old Bag who doesn't deserve saving! Eh?

An embarrassed pause

Well, you're right. All this time I've kept myself to myself and then complained that I was lonely. Stupid. I can see that now.
Salt Well, ma'am. Crisis brings folk together, so they say! (*He offers his hand*)
Old Bag Thank you.

Salt and the Old Bag shake hands. A sickly groan comes from Herr Von Cuckoo

Pepper I hate to interrupt your touching little scene, but Cuckoo is getting worse.
Salt I'm sorry, Miss Pepper. Excuse me, ma'am.

Salt hastens to help, leaving the Old Bag on her own, thinking

Old Bag (*after a pause, whispering to the shelf above*) Psst. Gingerbread Man.
Gingerbread Man Yes.
Old Bag You said that bird was poisoned?
Gingerbread Man By the Big Ones. And they'll chuck him in the Dustbin if he's not better when they come down. But, as you said, his cuckoos are very noisy. Good riddance.

Pause. Salt and Pepper, who have heard this exchange, look on in anticipation

Old Bag (*to everybody*) May I examine Herr Von Cuckoo? I may be able to help.

Music starts as the Old Bag goes and looks at Herr Von Cuckoo. Then after a quick examination

Song 8 HERBAL REMEDY

Old Bag I can cure this malady
With a pure herbal remedy
I will effect it
With expedience
When you've collected
The ingredients.

Dill
Helps you sleep when you're ill
Horseradish
Eradicates the pain
Sage
Helps you live to old age
Rosemary
Strengthens the brain.

Chives
Are the saver of lives

Sweet Basil
A pow'rful antedote
Bay
Makes the aches go away
Bilberry
Soothes a sore throat.
Thyme
Puts you back in your prime
Witch Hazel
The antiseptic brew
Mint
Gives the eyes a fresh glint
Cinnamon
Fends off the 'flu.

All Dill, Horseradish, Sage, Rosemary,
Chives, Sweet Basil, Bay, Bilberry,
Thyme, Witch Hazel, Mint, Cinnamon

Old Bag Tarragon, and lastly
Parsley.

The music continues. Herr Von Cuckoo groans and writhes with pain

Old Bag (*rushing to him*) It's all right, Herr Von Cuckoo.

Herr Von Cuckoo raises his head and sees who it is. He groans even louder—in horror and fright; he knows how unpleasant the Old Bag can be

(*Calming him*) Don't flap! I'll get your voice back for you—(*turning from him; in a cross sotto voce*)—even if it *does* upset my nerves.

Herr Von Cuckoo half sits up, having heard this remark. He looks, with inquisitive worry

(*Correcting herself*) I said—I'll just get my herbs...

Herr Von Cuckoo is satisfied by this and lies flat again. The song continues. During the next section, the Gingerbread Man throws down the ingredients; the others place them in the egg cup which they drag forward for the purpose. (N.B. In the first production, Salt, Pepper and the Gingerbread Man all went to the top shelf (using the back entrance) and sang the names of the herbs as solo lines while finding the herbs and putting them in the egg cup, which the Old Bag handed up to them. The Old Bag therefore sang the lines describing the herbs' properties. This may or may not be practical in other productions)

Gingerbread Man Dill
All Helps you sleep when you're ill
Gingerbread Man Horseradish
All Eradicates the pain
Gingerbread Man Sage
All Helps you live to old age

Gingerbread Man Rosemary
All Strengthens the brain.

Gingerbread Man Chives
All Are the saver of lives
Gingerbread Man Sweet Basil
All A pow'rful antidote
Gingerbread Man Bay
All Makes the aches go away
Gingerbread Man Bilberry
All Soothes a sore throat.

Gingerbread Man Thyme
All Puts you back in your prime
Gingerbread Man Witch Hazel
All The antiseptic brew
Gingerbread Man Mint
All Gives the eyes a fresh glint
Gingerbread Man Cinnamon
All Fends off the 'flu.

Old Bag A final touch of Tarragon
Soon you'll be the paragon
Of health, once again, fighting fit.

Lastly
Pass me
The Parsley ...

The Gingerbread Man throws it. The Old Bag adds it to the other ingredients

That's it!

Old Bag It is ready. Herr Von Cuckoo must now drink.

Tension music as Salt and Pepper help Herr Von Cuckoo up and lead him to the egg cup. The Gingerbread Man watches from the shelf above

Salt Come on, shipmate.

Herr Von Cuckoo groans

Pepper Drink this, Cuckoo.

Herr Von Cuckoo recoils from the smell of the brew

Herr Von Cuckoo Ugh!
Old Bag The nastier it smells, the more good it does you. Drink. It will make you sleepy.

Herr Von Cuckoo drinks, helped by the others. He makes faces at the taste

Do you feel sleepy?

Herr Von Cuckoo shakes his head and shrugs his shoulders. Then suddenly he relaxes into sleep as if by magic

That's good. Mr Salt, please help me lead him home.

Salt Aye, aye, ma'am.

They set off for the clock

Pepper Will he get better?
Old Bag I think so. But not for a few hours. I'll stay with him.
Salt As long as he's shipshape by eight o'clock. The Big Ones will be down by then. They'll expect to hear him cuckoo.
Old Bag I'll do my best.
Salt Thank you, Old Bag.
Old Bag Thank me when he's better.

The Old Bag takes Herr Von Cuckoo inside. The door shuts. Salt returns to Pepper

Salt Well, Miss Pepper, something exciting, out of the ordinary; that's what you wanted.
Pepper And that's what I've had. Those shivers of terror. That awful uncertainty. The dreadful frights. My, it's been a wonderful night. (*She grins*) I do hope it hasn't finished yet!
Gingerbread Man (*from the shelf above*) It's hardly started!

Salt and Pepper jump

Salt Ah! (*Looking up*) It's only Gingerbread Man.
Pepper Oh. You made me jump. How delicious! I'd forgotten you were up there.
Gingerbread Man You've forgotten something else as well.
Pepper What's that?
Gingerbread Man Sleek the Mouse is up here too! (*He indicates the teapot*) In there.
Salt Can't we leave him there?
Gingerbread Man In the Old Bag's teapot?
Pepper Give him the poison.
Gingerbread Man He wouldn't fall for that. He saw it being put down.
Pepper You'll just have to let him out and order him home.
Gingerbread Man I can't do that. He's starving. He won't stop to listen. He'll just start nibbling. Me.
Salt Where does he live, anyway?
Gingerbread Man Behind the dresser. (*He has an idea.*) Wait a minute. He's only here because I was curious and let him in. If we could get him back through this hole (*indicating the hole on the shelf*), block it up, *and* push the plate back down below, he'd be shut out.
Salt He'd never fall for that! You just said, he's starving. He won't disembark from this dresser till he's had his nibble.
Gingerbread Man Well, he's not nibbling *me.*
Pepper No. We won't let him. We'll have to catch him and *then* force him back through the hole.
Salt But how?

All think and look around

Gingerbread Man (*Suddenly*) Your mug!
Salt (*Thinking he means "face"*) What?
Gingerbread Man Your mug!
Salt What about it?
Gingerbread Man It's big enough.
Salt Are you being cheeky?
Gingerbread Man No. You've got a big mug.
Salt How dare you?
Gingerbread Man Over there. (*He points*) We could use it.
Salt Oh. *That* mug.
Gingerbread Man Yes. When he comes down, drop it over him.
Pepper Yes, that could work. (*She goes to fetch the mug*) Then push him to the hole, let him go through and block it up again. How thrilling!
Gingerbread Man Exactly.
Pepper But how do we drop the mug over him? He'll see it coming.

Pause

Salt Got it. Watch, shipmates!

Music, as Salt takes the string from the rolling pin and attaches it to the handle of the upturned mug. He then mimes to the Gingerbread Man to throw down the sling hoist end, keeping the rope passing over the hook (or another hook if this is more convenient). By hauling on the string, the mug will rise—at least, the handle *side will, leaving the opposite side still on the deck*

(*Excitedly*) Demonstration.
Gingerbread Man Roll up, roll up. See Mr Salt's Patent Mug Mouse Trap.
Music, as Salt pulls the string, and makes the mug rise

Salt Now, Miss Pepper, could you hang onto the halyard please.
Pepper Certainly. What do I do?
Salt Nothing, ma'am, till I give the order. Then let down the mug.
Pepper I hope I don't get too excited.
Salt Now, I'm Sleek.

Tension music, as Salt goes to his starting position and does a Sleek impersonation, sniffing towards the mug

Okay, you guys, I'm the boss around here. Go, Miss Pepper!

Salt stands under the inverted mug. Pepper lets the string up, which brings the mug down over Salt.

Gingerbread Man Bravo, bravo. (*He applauds from the shelf above*)
Pepper Congratulations Mr Salt. (*She comes forward, leaving the string, and joins the applause*)
Salt Hey! Let me out!
Pepper Oh! (*Loudly*) Sorry.

She returns to the string, pulls, the mug rises, Salt comes out

Salt Right. Let him out, Gingerbread Man, and I'll stand by on the Mug Trap.
Gingerbread Man Hang on.
Salt Exactly. Hang on the halyard.
Gingerbread Man No. Hang on. Problem.
Salt Problem?
Gingerbread Man How do we make sure Sleek gets in the right position for the trap to work?
Pepper He's right. We can't just expect Sleek to happen to arrive there.

Pause

Gingerbread Man (*taking in the audience*) Any ideas? What would make Sleek want to go under the mug?

Audience participation should produce the idea of food. Sleek is hungry and the scent of food would lead him anywhere. This section, led by the Gingerbread Man, will have to be improvized, depending upon the reactions and ideas of the audience. Hopefully, having established the "food" idea, the next stage is "what sort of food?" The audience should be guided towards the idea of something sweet—sweets!

Gingerbread Man Of course! Sweets. A sweet under the mug! Salt. Any sweets on the dresser?
Salt Sorry, shipmate.
Gingerbread Man Has *anyone* got a sweet we could use? Wrapped or unwrapped! Chocolate or boiled! Hands up. Don't throw them. Miss Pepper, perhaps you could select one!
Pepper Certainly. Now, let's see. (*She looks at the audience, and selects a donor*) You. Could we use your sweet?... Thank you. Can you throw it to me? (*She receives it*) Oh yes, this should work. It looks very tempting. Smells it too. (*She describes the sweet*)
Salt Right, Miss Pepper. Under the mug. Heave ho!

Salt raises the mug, and Pepper carefully positions the sweet

Pepper Ready.
Salt Gingerbread Man, let him out!
Gingerbread Man Hang on.
Salt Again?
Gingerbread Man Yes. We need something else to make the plan foolproof.
Salt Go on then.
Gingerbread Man Something to make sure that Sleek doesn't fool us by grabbing the sweet very quickly—before the mug has time to catch him.
Salt Yes. Something to make him freeze, still as a statue, perhaps.
Pepper Of course! He did that when the Big Ones came in.
Salt What?
Pepper Stood transfixed. They were shouting at him.
Gingerbread Man What were they shouting?
Pepper Well, *she* was screaming and *he* was going "Shoo, shoo, shoo!"
Gingerbread Man That's it, then. We'll shout at him.

Salt I doubt if we can shout as loud as the Big Ones ...
Gingerbread Man Perhaps—(*to the audience*)—would *you* help us again? You will? Thank you.
Pepper Splendid. Now, if all the ladies and girls could scream very loudly, the moment Sleek arrives under the mug ...
Salt I could use my whistle as a signal!
Pepper Yes.
Salt And at the same time, if all the gentlemen and boys could go—"Shoo, shoo, shoo"—yes? Let's try it. All together. After the whistle.
Pepper I'll pretend to be Sleek.

Pepper acts as Sleek approaching the mug. Salt blows his whistle. The audience practice their noises and Salt encourages. Pepper acts transfixed

(*When satisfied*) Thank you. Excellent.
Salt (*Manning the string*) Ahoy there, Gingerbread Man. Let him out!

Salt hauls up the mug. Tension

Gingerbread Man (*breaking the tension*) Hang on!
Salt Not again!
Gingerbread Man Last time.
Pepper Go on, then.
Gingerbread Man Well, if—(*indicating the audience*)—everybody is going to be kind enough to help us, we ought to make sure they're protected.
Salt How do you mean?
Gingerbread Man Suppose Sleek decides to leave the dresser and invade *them?*

Pause

Pepper Got it! When he goes to the mug, they—(*indicating the audience*)—make him freeze; if he goes to the edge— *I* make him *sneeze*! Mr Salt! Twist my grinder!
Salt Oh, Miss Pepper. You're hot stuff!

Song 9 HOT STUFF

During the song, Salt and Pepper place pepper all around the edge of the dresser, and Salt acts out the effects of pepper mentioned in the lyrics.

Pepper I can make you sneeze
Like a tickle with a feather
I can make you sneeze
Like a change of weather
I can make you sneeze
Just a sniff's enough
Ev'ryone agrees
I'm
Hot stuff.

I can make you sneeze
Like a duster that is dusty

Splutter like a breeze
When it blows up gusty
I can make you sneeze
With a huff and puff
Ev'ryone agrees
I'm
Hot stuff.

First your nose will itch
On your brow a puzzled frown
Then your nose will twitch
Atishoo atishoo
And all fall down.

I can make you sneeze
Like the pollen in the summer
Ev'ryone agrees
I'm a red hot Momma
I can make you sneeze
Like a pinch of snuff
Ev'ryone agrees
I can make you sneeze
Make you cough and make you wheeze
Ev'ryone agrees
I'm
Hot stuff.

Atishoo!

Salt Gingerbread Man, can we set sail now?
Gingerbread Man Aye, aye sir! You two keep out of sight as much as you can. (*To the audience*) And don't forget, everybody ...

Pepper screams to remind the audience of the plan

Salt Shoo, shoo, shoo.
Gingerbread Man When you hear the whistle. Good luck.

Tension music, as the Gingerbread Man creeps to the teapot, removes whatever he has blocked the door with, and gingerly opens the door an inch; then he runs to hide. Below, all is set; Salt has hauled on the string, the mug is in the up position; and the sweet is in position. Pause.

Suddenly, Sleek the Mouse enters

Sleek Okay, Ginger, I've had enough of your tricks. Prepare to beat your maker—prepare to meet your baker ... (*He sees the audience*) And as for you—you're the creepiest, crawliest critters I've ever sniffed. Did you stop laughing at me when I asked? Not on your life! When Ginger shut me up, did you warn me? Not on your life! And do you think I'm gonna

forgive and forget? Not on your life! You've asked for a sweetie raid and a sweetie raid you're gonna get. I'm coming down! Yes I am!
Audience No you're not!
Sleek Oh yes I am!
Audience Oh no you're not!
Sleek Oh yes I am!
Audience Oh no you're not!
Sleek You just watch this!

Sleek jumps, or slides down, from the shelf to the stage level. The Gingerbread Man, during the following action, peeps out from hiding to survey the scene

Sweetie raid! (*He advances towards the audience, sniffing all the while*) You just rustle 'em up ready or I'll nibble *you* instead. Mmmm. Caramel whirls, fruit gums, gob stoppers ... (*He reaches the edge of the dresser, sniffs and* ...) A ... a ... a ... tishoo! (*He backs away a little, then comes forward, at a different angle.*) Chewy bullseyes, liquorice sticks, peppermints ... (*The sniffing of pepper is repeated.*) A ... a ... a ... tishoo! (*He backs away again, chooses another angle to go. As he starts, he suddenly reacts to a new scent, and stands, excitedly sniffing and trying to place the smell*) Oh! That sure is a swell smell! Kind of juicy and crunchy and—(*etc., improvizing to describe the type of sweet under the mug—which will vary from performance to performance*)— my favourite sweetie! Where is it, where is it?

The audience should lead Sleek to the mug. He can veer the wrong way a couple of times, but eventually he reaches the mug, and spots the sweet

Mmmmm! There it is! (*He starts to creep under the mug, then stops*) This isn't a trick is it?
Audience (*encouraged by the Gingerbread Man above*) No.
Sleek It's not a trap?
Audience No.
Sleek 'Cos if it *is*—you've had it!

The tension music builds as Sleek tentatively goes under the mug and reaches for the sweet. At the appropriate moment, Salt blows his whistle

Audience (*Encouraged by the Gingerbread Man above*) Aaaaaah! Shoo, shoo! Aaaaaah. Shoo, shoo! etc.

Sleek, as expected, reacts by staring transfixed. After enough time to establish this, Salt lowers the mug, enveloping Sleek. Salt, Pepper and the Gingerbread Man cheer

Gingerbread Man Well done, everyone! Thank you.

Music continues as Salt and Pepper push the mug to the corner, where the hole is, and carefully line it up in the correct position. The Gingerbread Man watches, excited, from above. Suddenly Salt has a thought and indicates to the Gingerbread Man to cover the hole on the shelf. The Gingerbread Man does this, using the matchbox and the honey pot. Then he jumps down below and helps Salt and Pepper to gently tip back the mug. After a pause we see Sleek the Mouse emerge. Salt blows his whistle again, the audience do their noises,

Sleek reacts and runs to and through the hole. The Gingerbread Man slides the plate to its original position. All is safe. All cheer. Victory! They shake hands and thank the audience for their help

The door of the cuckoo clock opens, and the Old Bag comes out

Old Bag Shhhh! Quiet! Herr Von Cuckoo is asleep.
Gingerbread Man Sleek's gone home!
Old Bag My home?
Gingerbread Man No, behind the dresser.
Old Bag Good riddance.
Salt How is Cuckoo?
Old Bag Much better. But he must have hush. If he can sleep till just before eight o'clock he should be fine again.
Pepper And his cuckoos?
Old Bag Back to their irritating, noisy selves!
Gingerbread Man Hooray!
Salt, Pepper / **Old Bag** Shhh! *speaking together*

Song 10 COME THE LIGHT

Salt, Pepper, the Gingerbread Man, and the Old Bag

Come the light
The light of day
The problems of the night
Will fade away
Faint ray of hope
May you shine bright
Making ev'rything come right
Come the light.

Hear the tick tick tock
Of the cuckoo clock
Ticka taking us toward the dawn
Hear the time tick by
Hear the seconds fly
Ticka telling us tomorrow's born.

And
Come the light
The light of day
The problems of the night
Will fade away
Faint ray of hope
May you shine bright
Making ev'rything come right
Come the light.

Hear the tick tick tock
Of the cuckoo clock
Ticka tocka never going wrong
Hear the time tick by
Hear the seconds fly
Ticka telling us it won't be long.

And
Come the light
The light of day
The problems of the night
Will fade away
Faint ray of hope
May you shine bright
Making ev'rything come right
Come the light.

Come the light
Come the light,
May ev'rything come right
Come the light.

At the end of the song, they all fall fast asleep

Tick-tocking music is heard, to suggest a time lapse. If possible, the lighting narrows to the face of the cuckoo clock, where the hands turn round till they reach about ten minutes to eight. (During the next scene they creep up to eight o'clock.) The lighting changes to suggest the early morning. Salt, Pepper, the Gingerbread Man and the Old Bag are still asleep

The music continues as the door of the cuckoo clock opens, and Herr Von Cuckoo emerges, yawning and tentative at first, as though testing himself to make sure he is better. He checks the time on the clock face. He clears his throat …

Herr Von Cuckoo Mi, mi, mi, mi. (*He is pleased. He yodels—without difficulty*) La, la, la, la, la, te, teeeee. (*He smiles, delighted. Then, as a final test, he sings*) Cuck—oo! Cu—ckoo! (*They sound back to normal*) Ze toad has flown! My voice is found!

Song 10A TOAD IN THE THROAT (*reprise*)

Herr Von Cuckoo I was made in the mountains of Switzerland
(*yodel*)
From a fine piece of pine I was carved by hand
(*yodel*)
With all
My power
I call

The hour
On a clear and unwavering note
It's my
Belief
To my
Relief—
I haven't a toad in my throat.

(*Yodelling chorus*)

During the chorus, the others wake up, and, pleased and relieved to see Herr Von Cuckoo is better, gather round the clock. The music continues as they applaud him. He sees them

Herr Von Cuckoo My friends. Ich danke you much for better me making. (*He bows politely*)
Gingerbread Man (*Indicating the audience*) *Everybody* helped.
Herr Von Cuckoo (*To the audience*) My friends. Ich danke too you. (*He bows to the audience*) Ich would like to danke you all, as is ze custom in Switzerland, by inviting you all to join me in my yodel! You all will do zat, ja?
All including audience Ja/yes!
Herr Von Cuckoo Danke. After drei—three. Ein, zwei, drei...

All sing the yodelling chorus—those on stage should find it difficult. The audience will probably not be very good either! ...

(*After a while*) Nein, nein, nein. Das ist *horrible*! Listen, I teach you.
Herr Von Cuckoo teaches everyone line by line. If it is thought desirable, he could pull down a roller-blind-style song sheet from above his door, with the "words" on it

Yodel oddle oddle
Yodel oddle oddle
Yo ho ho
Yodel oddle oddle
Yodel oddle oddle
Yo tee hee
Yodel oddle oddle
Yodel oddle oddle
Yo yoo hoo
Yodel oddle oddle
Yodel oddle oddle
Dee.

Depending on audience response, Herr Von Cuckoo leads everyone in the whole chorus, once or twice. He then sings a verse *to lead into a chorus sung by everyone. The audience are encouraged to cough and "Mi, Mi, Mi" before they sing*

Herr Von Cuckoo I was made in the mountains of Switzerland
(*Yodel*)

From a fine piece of pine I was carved by hand
(*Yodel*)
With all
My power
I call
The hour
On a clear and unwavering note
It's my
Belief
To my
Relief
I haven't a toad in my throat

Herr Von Cuckoo sings the chorus with the audience

Bravo, bravo.

All on stage clap the audience. Suddenly a loud door noise stops everyone in their tracks, and a bright light snapped on tells us that the Big Ones have arrived. Tension music. All scuttle to their number one positions—Herr Von Cuckoo in his clock, and Salt and Pepper below the shelf, if possible with the letter between them. The Gingerbread Man and the Old Bag both go behind the rolling pin—the Gingerbread Man flat out as he was at the beginning.

We hear the voices of the Big Ones. The clock points to eight o'clock. The shadows of the Big Ones are seen against the dresser

Mrs Big One Hurry up, dear. We'll be late.
Mr Big One Sorry darling, I must have overslept.
Mrs Big One Well, I've got to be at work by nine.
Mr Big One No time for breakfast then.
Mrs Big One Any sign of that mouse, dear?
Mr Big One No, darling, he wouldn't dare come back after the way we sent him packing last night!

Indignantly, the Gingerbread Man pops up for a second, as if to say "You sent him packing? We did!" *Realizing what he is doing, he stops and drops down again*

Mrs Big One Good.

Herr Von Cuckoo enters from his door, and with great confidence, proclaims the time

Herr Von Cuckoo Cuckoo! Cuckoo! Cuckoo! Cuckoo!
Cuckoo! Cuckoo! Cuckoo! Cuckoo!

He stands there, listening

Mr Big One Did you hear that, darling? Eight perfect working order cuckoos.
Mrs Big One He's not past it after all! No Dustbin for him!

Herr Von Cuckoo smiles radiantly. He has forgotten to go back inside

Mr Big One Probably a bit of fluff in his works.

Herr Von Cuckoo looks indignant

Come on, darling.
Mrs Big One Do you want the Gingerbread Man to nibble in the car?
Mr Big One That's an idea.

The Gingerbread Man's head emerges nervously from behind the rolling pin

Mrs Big One Otherwise your tummy will rumble, dear; no breakfast inside you.
Mr Big One Hang on. No. He's probably all germy—

The Gingerbread Man looks indignant

—that mouse's dirty paws must have run all over him.
Mrs Big One Ugh, you're right, dear. Don't eat him. Might make yourself ill.

The Gingerbread Man looks relieved. The Old Bag pops her head up to congratulate him

Mr Big One No. I'll throw him in the Dustbin.

Their reactions change to fright

Mrs Big One Oh no, don't do that. He's nice. He's got a cheeky face. Let's keep him—as a sort of decoration. He can stand on the shelf next to the tea pot. Come on, dear, we'll be late.

The bright light is switched off, and a door slam tells us the Big Ones have gone. Pause. Then all five emerge cheering, and converge centre, shaking hands with each other, and Herr Von Cuckoo kissing cheeks

Salt Congratulations, Cuckoo. You've never sung better.
Herr Von Cuckoo Danke. Danke you all.
Pepper Gingerbread Man ...
Gingerbread Man (*fiercely*) Don't come near me!
Pepper Why not?
Gingerbread Man (*laughing*) I'm germy and nasty and horrible—(*He jokingly advances on her like a monster*)

All laugh

—but I'm not to be beaten, and not to be eaten!
Salt A happy end to the voyage.
Old Bag (*angrily*) Happy? First that bird is better, and second, I have to share my shelf with *him*? (*She indicates the Gingerbread Man*) You think I'm *happy?* (*Awkward pause. Then she breaks into a huge smile*) I'm delighted, thrilled...!

The Gingerbread Man runs to the Old Bag

And if you don't visit me at least twice every day, there'll be trouble!

Gingerbread Man Trouble? I can cope with trouble. Your fortune telling was right.

Old Bag Of course!

Gingerbread Man "When trouble comes, if you can cope
Three lives will shortly find new hope."

Herr Von Cuckoo One is me. I escaped the Dustbin.

Gingerbread Man Two is me. I escaped a tummy!

Salt And three?

Old Bag Three is—me!

Pepper What did you escape?

Old Bag I escaped—from myself. And found you—my friends.

All cheer

Gingerbread Man Let's have a party! (*He goes to the transistor radio*)

Salt Now?

Pepper Why not? A celebration. To celebrate the first day of excitement on this dresser I can remember. The day that began…

All (*Except the Gingerbread Man*) With the Gingerbread Man!

Salt Hip, hip.

All Hooray.

Pepper Hip, hip.

All Hooray.

Herr Von Cuckoo Hip, hip.

All Hooray.

The Gingerbread Man turns on the transistor radio. The music starts and all sing and dance

Song 10B THE GINGERBREAD MAN (*reprise*)

Pepper Ginger
Salt Ginger
Old Bag Ginger
Her Von Cuckoo Ginger
Gingerbread Man Ginger?
All Ginger, ginger,
Gingerbread Man.

Soon as you arrived the
Dresser party began
Hey hey
You're the Gingerbread Man
Ginger you're the greatest
I'm your number one fan
Hey hey
You're the ginger, ginger
Ginger, ginger, ginger
Ginger, ginger
Gingerbread Man.

Ginger, ginger
Ginger, ginger, ginger
Ginger, ginger
Gingerbread Man.

Gingerbread Man Newly baked this morning
Take a look at my/his tan
Hey hey
I'm the Gingerbread Man
Like a magic spell I
Just appeared with a bang
Hey, hey
I'm the ginger

All Ginger

Gingerbread Man Ginger

All Ginger

Gingerbread Man Ginger

All Ginger

Gingerbread Man Ginger, ginger,
Gingerbread Man.

All Ginger, ginger,
Ginger, ginger, ginger
Ginger, ginger
Gingerbread Man.

Gingerbread Man One more time

All Ginger, ginger
Ginger, ginger, ginger
Ginger, ginger
Gingerbread Man.

The music continues as all the characters return to their places on the dresser: (N.B. It may be too difficult for the Old Bag and the Gingerbread Man to reach the shelf—if so, they can remain below)

Final tableau

CURTAIN

Photo: John Seymour

Susie Caulcutt's design for the original production.

FURNITURE AND PROPERTY LIST

On stage: GENERAL NOTE: All the characters are supposed to be only a few inches high. All properties and furnishings, therefore, are made large-scale to match. Most can be fairly simply cut-outs.

2 plates
Mug
Tin (optional). *In it:* length of string
Sugar bowl with several lumps of sugar
Egg cup
Transistor radio
Cottage-style teapot with practical door
Several herb jars
Pot of honey
Cuckoo-clock with practical door
Rolling-pin. *Behind it:* various pieces of currant and peel
Tea-cloth
Cup-hooks
Large envelope

Personal:

Salt: whistle
Herr Von Cuckoo: handkerchief

LIGHTING PLOT

Property fittings required: nil

Interior. A Dresser. The same scene throughout

ACT I

To open: Suggestion of bright moonlight—as this is the lighting for most of the play, it must be clear enough for the whole set to be visible

Cue 1 After door slams (Page 13)
Bring up blinding lighting, with shadow effect of the **Big Ones**

Cue 2 **Mrs Big One:** "... better than that." (Page 14)
Return to opening lighting

Cue 3 **Gingerbread Man** waves to **Salt** and **Pepper** (Page 19)
Restrict lighting to shelf area

Cue 4 **Gingerbread Man**: "Psssst. Salty" (Page 23)
Return to opening lighting

Cue 5 After door opens (Page 28)
Repeat Cue 1

Cue 6	**Mrs Big One:** "... in the morning, dear." *Return to opening lighting*	(Page 28)
ACT II		
To open:	As close of previous Act	
Cue 7	At end of Song 10 *Concentrate lighting on cuckoo-clock as hands change, then bring up general lighting to suggest early morning*	(Page 45)
Cue 8	At end of yodelling song (10A) *Repeat Cue* 1	(Page 47)
Cue 9	**Mrs Big One:** "... we'll be late." *Return to opening lighting*	(Page 48)

EFFECTS PLOT

ACT I

Cue 1	As CURTAIN rises *Sound of ticking clock*	(Page 1)
Cue 2	**Salt:** "That was invigorating!" All dance *Sound of door opening*	(Page 13)
Cue 3	After lights return to normal *Door slam*	(Page 14)
Cue 4	As **Gingerbread Man** approaches **Salt** and **Pepper** *Loud scratching, scuffling noise*	(Page 25)
Cue 5	After "mini chase" starts *Sound of door opening*	(Page 28)
Cue 6	**Mr Big One:** "... some poison down." *Sounds of cupboard door and tin opening*	(Page 28)
Cue 7	**Mrs Big One:** "... in the morning, dear." *Door slam*	(Page 28)

ACT II

Cue 8	At end of yodelling song *Sound of door opening*	(Page 47)
Cue 9	**Mrs Big One:** "... we'll be late." *Door slam*	(Page 48)